CONTENTS

First published 2018
Copyright © 2018 The General of The Salvation Army
ISBN 978-1-911148-61-3
e-book ISBN 978-1-911148-62-0
Design: Jooles Tostevin
Project editor: Paul Mortlock

A catalogue record of this book is available from the British Library

Bible references are from the *New International Version UK 2011*,
except if indicated otherwise

Published as part of the OneArmy series by
The Salvation Army International Headquarters
101 Queen Victoria Street, London EC4V 4EH
United Kingdom

Printed and bound in the UK by Page Bros, Norwich

As well as having the benefit of being brief and easy to read, *Who is this Jesus anyway?* also provides a wealth of stimulus for individual reflection. Its 'Face the Facts' reflections are designed to help readers think through their personal responses, and the provision of more than 200 Scripture references ensures there is plenty of detail to put each chapter into context.

Meeting together and discussing points raised can be particularly rewarding. We each have different ways of looking at things and are at various stages on our life's journey. As such, we have opportunity to learn from one another and contribute to the wider group. There is always more to discover. It is worth the extra effort.

Groups that take time to link the listed Scripture references with the main text will see how this exercise gives deeper insights into who Jesus was, what motivated his life and teaching, and what his priorities are for all time.

Individually or together, take time to see how the Bible gives us facts. Enjoy getting to know Jesus.

> "Meeting together and discussing points raised can be particularly rewarding. We each have different ways of looking at things and are at various stages on our life's journey."

Some Questions

- If there were a god – just the one – wouldn't that god want to create something?

- And wouldn't it make sense if that creation were able to relate to that god?

- Because it wouldn't make sense for that god to create something just so that god could feel important, would it?

- Because if that god created something, wouldn't it be for a specific purpose?

- And wouldn't that god want to create a life form that could have relationship with that god?

- So if that god created people for relationship, wouldn't that god decide to give people free will?

- But wouldn't this open the door for things to go wrong?

- And wouldn't that god's creation make bad choices as well as good?

- And relationships become a problem as a consequence?

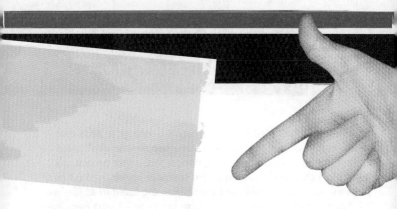

- Well, yes …

- But without free will would there be any meaning to anything?

- Because the creator god, more than anyone, would know that relationships need to be real – and genuine – or what is the point?

- So how might that god deal with this?

- And how might creation get the most helpful picture of that god?

- And what that god intends?

- And realise the reason for which it was made?

- Would God in human form help?

- ENTER JESUS.

JESUS IS A FACT

In an age filled with ready information, it is strange to note that within in all walks of life there are some people who don't seem to realise that Jesus Christ is an historical fact – that he actually lived. Even though the Common Era calendar begins from his birth (AD Anno Domini) and the centuries before are listed as BC (Before Christ), the fact of his life – and its impact since – hasn't been fully grasped by a surprising number of people.

MOST OF US notice the things that interest us and manage not to notice the things that don't. It's natural. Usually we aren't even aware that we are doing it. We just make automatic responses to things that come our way. Sports, finance, animals, music, technology, health – we make our responses according to our interest or situation. Mention of the name 'Jesus' brings automatic responses too. They range from being enthusiastically positive to strongly negative, with a variety of cursory or indifferent reactions in between.

For some, mention of the name 'Jesus' is taboo, and they never get round to finding out anything about him. There are plenty of reasons for this. Some have experienced bad examples of 'Christians' or encountered over-zealous evangelism, and then reacted with annoyance. Others assume the Bible is full of 'fairy stories' and include Jesus in a sweeping, unconsidered dismissal. Some may even think 'science' has disproved 'religion' and get no further than that – without noting that countless scientists are Christians.

Negative responses to Jesus can be picked up in many ways – at home, from parents who like to be self-contained or self-sufficient, or through a range of circumstances, including cultural influences, 'following the crowd', over-developed scepticism, bitterness, or not wanting to appear too religious. Alternatively, others are encouraged to love and trust Jesus from early days and then continue to do so, seeing it all as a natural, fulfilling way of life.

Whatever the case, it makes sense to begin by acknowledging that Jesus lived.[1] He is an historical fact. More than that, there was something sufficiently special about him for the world in general to date its calendar from the time of his birth. Obviously, this wouldn't have occurred if he had never lived, and only happened because of his universal following – a global impact made all the more remarkable because of the absence of mass media and other well-worn means of communication we take for granted today.[2]

We might justifiably expect these realities to stir some further thinking from us, but there is no guarantee they will. The human mind knows how to close itself to what it doesn't want to know or assumes doesn't matter. Life goes on. Its busyness claims our time, and other interests and duties make their claim. There is always something to distract us.

FACE THE FACTS

* Examine your 'automatic responses' in daily life.
* What do you notice? What do you ignore? And why?
* What has hindered or helped your recognising Jesus as a fact of life?

The four Gospels – of Matthew, Mark, Luke and John – have a convincing integrity of their own. They have a common theme about the nature of Jesus and events in his life, and they also have differences that broaden the picture, providing varied data that indicates they aren't the result of any collusion. Non-Christian historians such as Josephus and Tacitus, and Pliny, a Roman governor, make significant references to Jesus Christ. He lived.

THE FACT THAT the Gospels have survived in such compelling detail for more than 19 centuries, offers ready evidence of their timeless appeal. Something in their message speaks so well that countless translations and adaptations have been (and are increasingly being) made. They are trustworthy, historical documents in their own right, as are the Epistles – letters to churches – written by Christian leaders of the first century. Yet it is only by taking time to read them that their depth of human understanding, historical authenticity and challenge can be realised. The problem for many people is getting round to reading them.

Set within the historical and political context of the day, the Gospels highlight the significant roles of known Roman (Pontius Pilate) [1], Jewish (Herod Antipas)[2] and religious (Caiaphas)[3] leaders in the life of Jesus. Although historians have predictable, contrasting views on the characters involved, the place in history of these men is never in dispute. Gospel references, such as the death of Herod the Great[4] not long after the slaughter of baby

boys[5], confirms the focus well within known historical dates. Specific references to Jesus in first-century writings other than the Gospels, supply further evidence of his influence during this period. When the Roman historian Tacitus wrote of the Roman Emperor Nero's readiness to blame Christians for the fire that destroyed Rome in AD 64, he also recorded how 'Christus' had 'suffered the extreme penalty during the reign of Tiberius at the hands of … Pontius Pilatus'. The first-century Jewish historian Josephus in his *Jewish Antiquities*, included reference to James[6], as 'the brother of Jesus, the so-called Christ'. The reference compares with biblical data about James, especially in Paul's letter to the Galatians.[7] Yet the consistency and amount of detail contained in the Gospels themselves is more than sufficient to explain why Jesus hasn't been forgotten.[8]

While each Gospel has its own style, information and emphasis, they have a consistent unity of message. Their insights into the character of Jesus are never in conflict. As they take us on a path from his birth[9] to death[10] and Resurrection[11], we are introduced to someone who is like no other. His authority was matched by his humility, his leadership by his servanthood, his teaching by his example. He related to real people in real situations. He still does.

FACE THE FACTS

* What kind of thought have you previously given to Jesus?
* Assess your openness to reading the four Gospels (or just one Gospel) to gain an informed opinion on their value.
* Why might they have survived and been widely used to shape laws and attitudes throughout the past 2,000 years?

New Testament writings show how Christianity grew out of the conviction that the crucified Jesus had risen from the dead. They provide details of how Jesus' followers were so convinced of this that they were transformed from fearful, dejected losers into bold, world-changing ambassadors.

MEN WHO ARE dejected, bewildered, disillusioned, disarrayed and crushingly defeated in spirit don't turn into fearless, self-assured, pioneering, world-changing ambassadors without a reason – and the reason needs to be an overwhelmingly convincing one. It was.

The Gospels show, with clear, authentic narrative, how Jesus' followers found it difficult to understand the essence – the heart – of his teaching.[1] We can see indications that they were sometimes impressed, or even amazed, but as for grasping the implications of what he said – well, that wasn't always so easy for them. For example, his teaching on servanthood was contrary to their established views.[2] So it isn't surprising that, with great strength of feeling, they resisted any thought of his sacrifice and death.[3] Their view of the long-awaited Messiah had been one of glory and victory, not humiliation and defeat. They were reluctant to embrace a less attractive and more demanding path to glory – both for Jesus and themselves – and when Jesus was arrested, tried, tortured and killed, their world fell apart.[4]

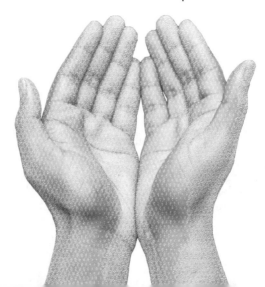

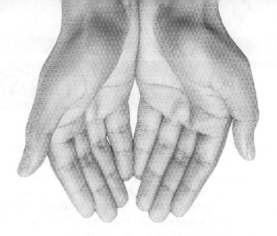

In spite of Jesus having told them he would 'rise again' they seem to have seen this as 'fancy tales'[5] and certainly failed to grasp the enormity of the information with which they had been entrusted.[6]

They were still lacking in trust after they first heard the news of the Resurrection.[7] It was too good to be true. But when Jesus presented himself to them on different occasions and in different locations they came to see and understand things differently.[8] Over a period of 40 days[9] they made adjustments to their thinking, slowly but surely absorbing the truth. Jesus, whom they and a host of others – soldiers, priests and bystanders – had seen die, had risen from the dead. His message that 'whoever believes in me shall have everlasting life'[10] had not been an idle boast or a flight of fancy. His Resurrection was a fact that opened new doors and possibilities for everyone.

It was also something that helped them open their hearts to welcome God's Spirit into the centre of their lives, to empower and direct them.[11] They became courageous, even fearless, in their proclamation of what they knew to be true.[12] They were utterly confident of their message. It coloured all their thinking, intensified every action. How could it be otherwise? They were changed people, transformed beyond recognition.

FACE THE FACTS
* Jesus' followers found some of his teaching conflicted with their preconceived ideas about God. How fixed are your views?
* Give some thought to what caused the disciples to change so dramatically.
* Would there have been a personal cost? If so, what would it have involved?

4 IT SHOWS LIFE'S REALITIES

The Gospels also show, in a natural way, how new Christians grappled with the implications of what their new-found faith meant for them. There is no attempt to present the growing number of Christians as perfect, and their inability to agree on some important issues highlighted the challenging reality of people from different backgrounds and cultures trying to work together. They were part of the real world. The same applies today.

THE DISCIPLES WERE changed people. They had fresh hopes, new aims and a message to transform anyone who would receive it. But the implications of their message, and the challenge of how to convey it, would tax the finest brains, bringing conflicts of opinion and convictions. They really did need God's guiding Spirit! They were human – just like us – with plenty of doubters ready to undermine their confidence and convictions. Their actions and reactions would be scrutinised by non-believers, as well as by fellow-believers whose culture and disposition meant they assessed matters differently.

At first the unity among believers astounded everyone. They even held 'all things in common'.[1] But as the number of followers grew, and towns and countries influenced by the 'new way'[2] increased, various interpretations of belief emerged. The implications and consequences of decisions had to be thought through – and from a universal perspective. The leaders needed clear heads, compassionate hearts and an openness to being guided by God into the new things he was doing.

It wasn't easy. The confidence and strength of purpose that comes with asking God to guide were both vital and welcomed – but they did not make anyone infallible. The disciples needed time to understand the wider picture. They needed patience, wisdom and the grace to admit when they may have got some things wrong. They were on an adventure, the like of which had never occurred before. Force and violence were not part of their agenda.[3] Love, example and sharing truth were required instead. Without these qualities they would not manage to represent or portray their Lord Jesus Christ in his true light.

Details of some of the disputes, decisions, poor behaviour and painful lessons that came with experience, make the New Testament alive with human drama.[4] They grant us glimpses into how Christianity spread in the early decades, what the setbacks were like, how progress came and how the message was agreed and developed. They also remind us that no church is ever composed of perfect people.[5] Our individual imperfections should help us understand that, and avoid any feelings of superiority. By virtue of Jesus' inclusive message, the early Christians were expected to make room for people who thought and sometimes acted differently from them.[6] The same principle still applies.

FACE THE FACTS

* How helpful is it that the New Testament doesn't hide the faults and disagreements of the early Christians?
* How realistic should we be about differences that may exist within and between churches and cultures today?
* Why do you think the Church grew so fast and spread so wide?

5 | JESUS DIED A YOUNG MAN

Jesus never became an old man. He died around 33 years old, crucified by the Romans, primarily because the Jewish religious authorities saw him as a threat.

IT ISN'T GOOD when you know people hate you – when people wish you harm or even that you didn't exist. It can make you uneasy and distracted. Does it make it easier or harder when you know the reason for their hatred? Jesus knew the reason why religious leaders hated him and he knew they wanted to kill him.[1]

No doubt some of them genuinely thought he was a blasphemer.[2] After all, he spoke as if he was God, and they saw him merely as a preacher from a northern village.[3] His teaching undermined their meticulously devised customs and traditions, without which they were likely to lose control of their authority.[4] They saw him as assaulting all they held dear.[5] In doing so, those who wanted him dead missed the point of his life and message. Strangely, it was the message they, like him, regarded as the most important – love God and one another.[6] But whereas they saw commands fulfilled through laws and rules, Jesus saw love as a matter of the heart. His teaching was filled with examples that showed he saw beyond the letter of the law and to the spirit of the law.[7]

Jesus knew matters would come to a climax. The authorities wouldn't allow him to continue his popular ministry unchecked.

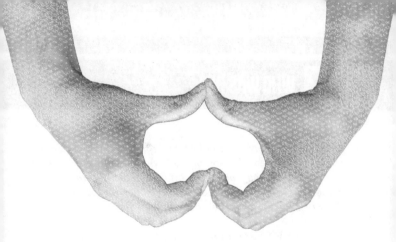

We aren't told in vast detail how Jesus coped with knowing he would die young or how he lived with the thought of the manner of his vicious and painful death – but we know he did.[8]

He found strength in prayer[9], especially on the night of the crucifixion.[10] He didn't want to die young, nor in the way that would unfold. If there was another way that could bring about the same result – the ultimate defeat of sin and death – he would readily have taken it. But there wasn't.[11]

He was utterly dedicated to living a life complete in love. He would not back out to save himself. Those who mocked him while he hung on the cross, challenged him to do so.[12] But, ironically, it was they – us – who needed saving and he had come to save. Nobody seemed to know that, or have any idea of what was about to be accomplished. Jesus did. He saw it through, fully expressing the 'greater love' of which he had earlier spoken.[13] And he died a young man.

FACE THE FACTS

*Why did religious leaders want Jesus out of the way?
*Why do you think Jesus didn't try to save himself from an early death?
*What is the difference between the letter of the law and the spirit of the law?

Known as the son of Mary and Joseph, Jesus eventually became recognised by many as the Son of God. Mary and Joseph were made aware of who he was before his birth. Their individual amazement at such unexpected responsibilities is recorded in Matthew and Luke – as is their obedience.

THE ASSERTION THAT Jesus is the Son of God is a matter of faith. It isn't something that can be proved by DNA or through a mathematical equation. There is no measuring facility for accurately defining what is human or divine. Attempting to separate them one from the other is also problematic. No one has the required insight to do so.

The Bible tells us that in Jesus, human and divine were inseparable. He was unique. John's Gospel describes him as the 'one and only'.[1] The detail John and other writers supplied of Jesus' life shows they had no doubts about this conclusion.[2]

Mary and Joseph didn't need to arrive at their own conclusions. They were told from the beginning that they were to be entrusted with bringing up the Son of God. When Mary was informed, by the angel Gabriel, that she would give birth to Jesus, she was (understandably) 'greatly troubled', yet she was also obedient.[3] Her life would never be the same again – and being pregnant before marriage would demand all the resources she could muster. She would be misjudged from the start.

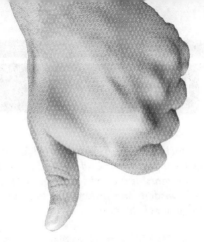

Joseph, required to act as father, didn't welcome the news. He too had to cope with a variety of emotions, not least the shocking news that Mary was pregnant – and being asked to believe this was all God's doing and for a divine purpose.[4] After reassurance by means of a dream, he came to terms with his role and seems to have given Mary all the support and protection she needed.

We have no record of how being given responsibility for Jesus affected them. On the one hand, it was an incomparable privilege. It was an affirmation of them as people. Great trust had been placed in them to guide the child in his early years. On the other hand, it would not be long before Jesus' understanding of life would be far in advance of theirs. His ministry would develop without their guidance. The latter years show Mary being corrected by Jesus[5] and, at the end, as a helpless spectator[6], with her Son making the life-surrendering decisions that would result in his cruel death.

As for who he was, his death and Resurrection have given the past 2,000 years a much fuller and informed perspective.

FACE THE FACTS

* Why can't the existence of God be proved or disproved by science or mathematical equation? Does it matter?
* What would help you most in your search for proof of God's existence and assessing who Jesus was?
* What kind of faith did Mary and Joseph need (individually and together) to carry through their God-given responsibilities of caring for Jesus through his young life?

HE WAS HUMAN

Although not much is known of Jesus' early life, Luke's Gospel shows he was keenly aware of God the Father's place in his life by the age of 12 years. It also tells us he grew as naturally as any other child – 'in wisdom and stature, and in favour with God and men'. He was genuinely human.

IT IS IMPORTANT to establish that Jesus was genuinely human. Luke's Gospel helps to authenticate this with a brief yet profoundly significant comment on Jesus' childhood. Luke covers almost his entire youth with one telling sentence – 'And Jesus grew in wisdom and stature, and in favour with God and man'.[1] In these words we see the natural human development of a child growing into adulthood.

The sentence is placed at the conclusion of a narrative about Jesus going to Jerusalem with his parents when he was 12 years old.[2] This is the only biblical insight given into Jesus' early years and it reveals that he possessed a lively mind, eager to discuss and debate – and to learn. Luke tells us that his meeting with teachers in the temple courts found him 'asking questions'. This was a sure way to grow in 'wisdom'. Luke is making the point that, even though he was divine, Jesus did not possess all knowledge. He didn't bring Heaven's hidden secrets with him! That would have made his life a sham. He had to learn and develop like the rest of us – and he did. This also explains why the choice of his parents was crucial. He had to be taught and nurtured in every good way.

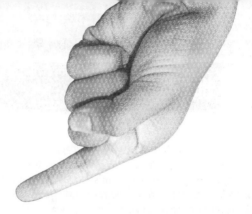

His growth in understanding would have gone alongside his growth in height. Growing 'in stature' is what all healthy children do and Jesus was no different. He experienced the varied stages of youth, learning how to handle his emotions and formulate appropriate responses to the experiences he encountered. All this would help in his growing 'in favour with men', taking his place in society in a positive way.

Growing 'in favour with God' is Luke's way of expressing that Jesus increasingly understood the divine will for his own life. As he did so, he began to recognise divine qualities within himself, eventually coming to realise who he was, and his unique role in the divine will and plan.[3] The Temple encounter with teachers as a boy shows that by the age of 12 Jesus was already giving thoughtful consideration to God the Father's place in his life. He not only asked questions, but also his understanding and answers left teachers in amazement and his parents 'astonished'.

By the time he was 30 years old, Jesus felt ready to present himself to the public and begin his ministry.[4]

FACE THE FACTS

* Why was it necessary for Jesus to 'grow up' as naturally as any other human being?
* What does Jesus 'asking questions' show about the genuine nature of his 'growing up'?
* How would you assess your own development in the four areas mentioned for Jesus – relationship with God, relationship with others, physical ability and growth in wisdom?

The Bible makes it plain that he was also God. His coming to earth was prophesied centuries before his birth and he is seen as the fulfilment of divine promise. Christians readily use the term God for Jesus, as well as for the Father, and for God's Spirit. It isn't surprising that the divine essence was evident in Jesus' life.

THOSE WHO WERE entrusted with announcing Jesus to the world – in written or spoken form – were convinced he was God.[1] For them, Jesus' conquering of death was not some vague hope or theory to hold onto in dark times, it was a glorious, life-changing, world-embracing, effective truth.[2] God himself had come to be with them in human form and accomplished for us what we could never accomplish on our own.[3] The theme of a risen Lord runs throughout the writings of the New Testament.

Many people had been close to Jesus and had witnessed his teaching and example at first hand. They had heard him speak about himself and seen him daily demonstrate the value of what he was saying. John didn't hesitate to describe Jesus as divine. He began his first Letter with, 'That which was from the beginning, which we have heard, which we have seen with our eyes, which we have looked at and our hands have touched – this we proclaim…'.[4] John knew what and who he was writing about and he knew how to express it. In his Gospel, his use of the term 'full of grace and truth' for Jesus[5], helps explain the way in which he observed the divine in Jesus. It isn't a description that could justifiably be given to anyone else. This man was like no other.

He resisted hype and celebrity status, and discouraged people from publicising his healing miracles.[6] His care for individuals was selfless and his engagement with people in need was powerfully effective, life-changing and life-enhancing.[7] He was genuine, through and through.

Although there were people who realised Jesus was someone special, it was only in retrospect that he was viewed as the fulfilment of Old Testament prophecy.[8] The servant nature of his character[9], his humble birth[10] and his kingship of peace[11] were eventually seen as ratification of what was predicted in Scripture and is still there for us to read.

We have already acknowledged Jesus' humanity. His divinity was seen, not in any show of omniscience or omnipresence – that didn't occur, because he was truly human – but simply by the person he was and by the way he lived. We might say he was recognised by those who had the openness to notice, and that his divinity was seen most clearly because of the *man* he was.

FACE THE FACTS

* What were the main factors in the New Testament writers concluding that Jesus was the Son of God? What kind of things might have convinced them?
* In what ways do you think Jesus may have been different from what people expected?
* What attributes would you look for in someone claiming to be God?

21

By the age of 30 Jesus had decided it was time to begin his ministry. He made a public identification with God in a ceremony at the River Jordan – away from religious officialdom – and received God the Father's blessing.

IT WILL ALWAYS be the case that Jesus is recognised as God only by those who have the openness to ask who he is. There is no shortcut that omits the humility of seeking. John the Baptist recognised the worth of Jesus before Jesus had become well known.[1] Each of the four Gospels records their meeting at the River Jordan.[2] It was highly significant, because it marked the beginning of Jesus' ministry.

John expressed misgivings about baptising Jesus. He had made a general call to repentance and people had flocked to respond. Jesus was different. He had no sins that required forgiveness, so when he presented himself for baptism, John was uncomfortable and said he was unworthy to baptise him. 'I need to be baptised by you,' he said. He was right, of course, but Jesus reassured him and they went ahead.[3] And so, Jesus announced his arrival by his own baptism. Only he fully understood the depth and significance of the occasion.

The Gospels record the Spirit of God 'descending on Jesus' in that moment and the blessing of God the Father being given. 'This is my Son, whom I love; with him I am well pleased'.[4] It is difficult to think of a higher or more reassuring accolade. Jesus had the

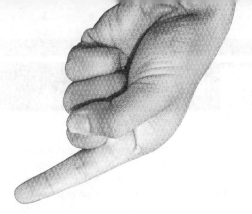

Father's full blessing on the mission on which he was about to embark. He couldn't do it without the assurance of God's Spirit within him. He now had that assurance and knew that he was equipped for what was ahead.

There was also a glimpse into the future. Jesus' welcoming of the Spirit would eventually lead to the possibility of anyone requesting the same source of empowerment. 'I baptise you with water,' said John, 'but he (Jesus) will baptise you with the Holy Spirit.'[5] God in man – relationship of relationships.

It is highly significant that all this took place away from religious officialdom.[6] Much as the 12-year-old Jesus had been energised by speaking with teachers in the temple courtyard, he was now distancing himself from a formal identification with religious authorities. He had taken time to observe issues that he thought should be addressed, such as established practices that were given an importance they didn't merit and attitudes that failed to show God's love. It was a distancing that would become increasingly apparent.

FACE THE FACTS

* Jesus made a public declaration of his own faith in God the Father. Why do you think he did so, and what value might similar public witness have today?
* Why do you think Jesus avoided identifying himself with the established religious authorities as he began his ministry?
* With the baptism of Jesus we have a glimpse of 'God in man'. How might God in us be of help?

HE TOOK TIME OUT

Following his baptism, Jesus spent some quiet time in the desert, praying and contemplating how he should proceed. Soon after, he chose the 12 men who would become his closest followers – the disciples. They were with him for the next three years.

HAVING RECEIVED unqualified affirmation from his Father, Jesus felt the need to think things through. He had no friend or acquaintance who was equipped to advise him on his forthcoming ministry, because no one was adequately aware of its extent or purpose. Jesus was alone in this – as he would be at the end. He took time out in the desert.[1] He wanted to be alone with his Father.

The implications of being God's Son – that was what the Father had called him – were immense. Could Jesus now accomplish 'anything'? What kind of power might he have? How should he present himself? What should or shouldn't he reveal about himself at this stage? How would people react to him? When and where should he start? These and other questions had to be faced. The Gospels give us an insight into how he handled them.

He retreated to the desert, where he became hungry. Perhaps he could turn stones into bread?[2] To do so would satisfy his own hunger (and allow special favours for himself), and possibly lead to feeding the poor and becoming a great hero. Similarly, to leap from

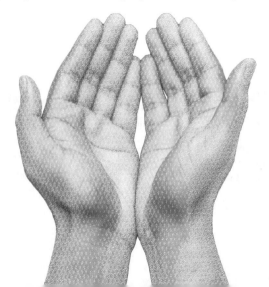

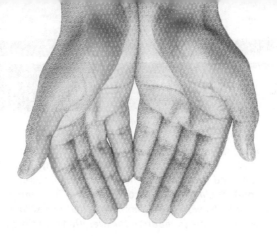

the Temple[3] – do something spectacular – would draw the crowds and ensure a swift following. Or he could make a pact with the devil, compromise on key issues without anyone knowing, and still appear powerful and successful.[4] He rejected each issue. He was better than that. What would be the point? People would follow for all the wrong reasons. The shortcuts wouldn't work – and were unworthy. They still are.

Had he chosen them, he couldn't have achieved what he had been sent to achieve. Popular acclaim can be encouraging, but it is cheap. Unless those he called offered honest response, genuine commitment and a willingness to give rather than take, any 'success' would be meaningless. These qualities mattered. They still matter. Jesus chose the harder path – and dedicated himself to giving all he was to all of us.[5]

Any disciples he might choose would need to embrace the same qualities. They wouldn't find it easy. They would learn as they went along. Jesus would observe their progress, study their reactions, offer encouragement and cope with their lack of ability to grasp basic truths. He chose 12 men – a mixed bunch.[6] The adventure had begun.

FACE THE FACTS

*What kind of things might Jesus have needed to think through when he took 'time out' in the desert?
* In what ways does it help that Jesus experienced temptation?
*Why would Jesus have been wary of popular acclaim?

When people first heard his teaching they described it as 'new' and were said to be amazed. The Gospels show why. They record Jesus rejecting and replacing old, harsh teaching by emphasising the values and teaching of a God of love. There is an integrity to all Jesus said. His words were both profound and simple, highlighting love as the foundation for everything that is good and lasting.

JESUS HAD AUTHORITY. It didn't come from qualifications. We know he had a lively mind and enjoyed studying and learning, but his authority didn't come simply from what he knew. It came from who he was – the person people could see. Mark's Gospel tells us that as soon as he began to teach, 'the people were amazed'.[1] The reason? 'He taught them as one who had authority, not as the teachers of the law'.[2] It seems that those with the official qualifications had something missing. They were lacking in what Jesus had. It was the vital ingredient – authenticity. Jesus lived by what he said. And what he said frequently exposed the misplaced priorities of the teachers.[3]

It must have been difficult – and annoying – for teachers to hear Jesus say, 'You have heard that it was said … but I tell you'. He is recorded as using the phrase a number of times.[4] No one had given him official permission to teach his own interpretation of the law, and then use it to replace what he thought needed updating. The teachers viewed him as undermining all they held dear.[5]

His use of questions helped people think for themselves[6] – not always welcomed by those who want to control other people. And even today, we find new thoughts and lessons from his down-to-earth parables.

Jesus had come to make a difference. He was there to correct misconceptions about the nature of God, what God required and the things in life that really mattered. The authorities needed to be challenged about the over-emphasis they were giving to ritual and procedure[7], and the lack of emphasis on care for the poor.[8] The poor and disadvantaged were not there to be looked down on or to make the well-off look important. Jesus described the poor – the sick, naked, hungry, homeless and in prison – as his 'brothers'.[9] They were to be helped. To ignore them was like ignoring the God in whose image they had been made. Think again about your priorities, said Jesus.

Keeping the law had become more important than caring for the people whom the law was intended to help. Everyone seemed agreed that the most important commandments were to love God and their neighbour, but it wasn't evident in the way things were prioritised. More lessons about love were needed.

FACE THE FACTS

* People saw Jesus as authentic. What might have been different about him and his teaching?
* How important do you think it was for him to correct misconceptions about God?
* What misconceptions about Jesus might exist today?

LOVE IS THE PRIORITY

Jesus affirmed that the two greatest commandments were to love God with heart, soul, mind and strength, and to love others as much as we love ourselves. By doing so he made our relationship with God the most important aspect of life. Every other priority or rule in life should be seen in the context of loving relationship.

THE WORD 'LOVE' can mean many things. English dictionary definitions range from 'have a great affection for' to 'a wholehearted liking for something', 'sexual passion' and 'enjoy very much'. They don't always include or refer to love being costly, often sacrificial and involving qualities of character rather than warm feelings. So when any of us use the word 'love', others don't always have the same understanding of what we mean by it. It covers so many areas of life.

When Jesus said that the two greatest commandments were to love God with heart, soul, mind and strength, and to love others as much as we love ourselves[1], he was speaking of love in the context of loyalty, faithfulness and companionship. It involves commitment, giving and receiving.

Love can't be measured, of course, and that may be one reason why it isn't easily defined. Yet when we read the apostle Paul's words to the Corinthians on love[2] we are left in no doubt about its supremacy in human interaction and relationship. Paul describes love as being patient and kind. It doesn't envy or boast, and neither is it proud. It isn't rude or self-seeking, not easily

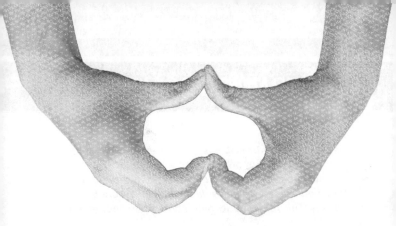

angered and keeps no score of wrongs. It protects, trusts, hopes and perseveres. He says much more too, yet this brief list of its qualities adequately tells us that when Jesus says we should put love at the heart of everything, he is talking about much more than affection or desire. He is pointing us to the source of all that is good in our world. In his first Letter, John describes God himself as love.[3] It all fits.

The love of God – its self-giving and all-embracing nature – was seen supremely in Jesus.[4] Even so, we have only been given a glimpse of its unfathomable depths.

Jesus kept his own commandments and showed why they matter. They provide the foundation for everything else in life. Keeping these two great commandments works. It makes relationships genuine and mutually beneficial.

Sometimes we suffer because of love – for doing what is right. Love isn't always appreciated or wanted. Depth of love can be followed by depth of disappointment, or of sorrow. Neither is happiness guaranteed, nor should it be the motivation for showing love. Yet the cohesion that love brings to our world is irreplaceable. And without it we are lost.

FACE THE FACTS

* Define for yourself what you think Jesus meant when he used the word 'love'.
* How essential is love?
* 'Love cannot be measured.' Of which other qualities can this be said? What is special about them?
  (It may be helpful to read 1 Corinthians chapter 13 to help with these reflections on love.)

29

13 RELATIONSHIP IS THE KEY

An essential guiding principle is that the greatest command is not for us to serve, worship or obey God – it is to love him. Serving, worshipping and obeying God may flow from this, but the prime emphasis on loving God helps us see him in a more personal, caring way. This relationship gives eternal perspective to life.

IT IS COMPARATIVELY easy to think in terms of worshipping a god. The created bowing before their creator is not a difficult concept, even for people who do not believe in God. But left there, the concept is inadequate – and it does God a disservice, misunderstanding his purposes for us. God offers us a relationship with him, something more personal, more intimate. We have noted that the two greatest commandments are to love God and others.[1] They are not to serve or worship God – even though these may be an integral part of our response to the Almighty. They are for us to love.

Being commanded to love can seem a strange concept. We don't warm to the idea of being instructed to genuinely express an emotion. It doesn't make sense. It can't be done. Yet when love is understood in the context of being loyal, faithful, committed, honest, selfless and giving – these are achieved through personal decision. And the decision we are invited to make by God is to show these qualities in relationship with him – and others. If our relationship with him is to be beneficial, to be worthwhile, it needs to be genuine, honest and open – rooted in love.

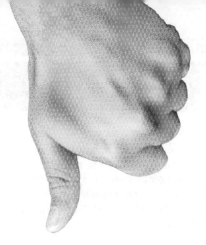

Relationships involve interaction, getting to know one another, meaning something to each other. When understood in the context of love, we see that our relationship with God is intended to be personal – to get to know him. He wants to be our friend![2] It shows that God is ready to share himself with us, inviting us to learn from him and, in so doing, also discover how to relate to one another.[3] We may even explore the possibility of becoming more like him – and when that process begins, we become more loving.[4] 'Love one another. As I have loved you, so you must love one other,' was the last commandment Jesus gave to his disciples.[5] When we try to put this command into action our world becomes a better place and we become better people. There is no better option.

Jesus chose to come to earth as a human being to help us see – through relationship – what God was like. God is not unfeeling, remote or uncaring. He came in Jesus to live among us[6], identifying fully with us, inviting us to get close to him. The invitation was personal – 'Follow me'.[7] It still is.

FACE THE FACTS

* As God has made love the greatest command, what does this say about his nature and the possibility of relationship with him?
* How does Jesus help us understand better the role and significance of love in human life and action?

Some people become nervous or suspicious at the thought of talking with God. They haven't managed to see it in its natural context and may have been put off by some ill-informed comments. It isn't weird or strange. It is as natural as breathing and is best seen as a normal part of life. A developing relationship with God can bring added wisdom and insight too.

PRAYER IS BEST understood as talking with God. Set within the context of relationship it becomes a normal part of life and is two-way. It is designed to be natural and enriching. When Jesus gave teaching on prayer – at the request of his disciples – he encouraged them to address God as 'Father'.[1] Talking with God should be like talking with a caring parent. Prayer doesn't have to be formal. God has many attributes and is called by many names, but Jesus didn't want these to get in the way of the intimate, open, developing relationship God wants for us.

Prayer makes sense. It would be strange – and illogical – for God to create us with a capacity for relationship and never make use of it. Take relationships away and life has little if any meaning. If we weren't able to communicate with God, nor he with us, what would be the point of his creating us? As we have already noted, Jesus stressed that God's number one priority for us is to love him and others[2] – and prayer gives opportunity to reflect on this.

It doesn't take a great deal of observation to notice that people have different approaches to prayer. Culture, upbringing and

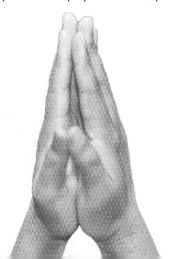

personal disposition play their part in this. God hasn't laid down procedural rules for prayer. He has his own way of being to us just what we each need. All that is required from us is an open, sincere approach to talking with him.[3] Without this there is no point in proceeding anyway. God can only help us – add to our lives, help us develop our understanding – if we are honest with him and ourselves. It is often in the quiet, unhurried moments we give to prayer that we understand best what God is wanting us to hear.

Prayer is a privilege. It is a means by which we can become aware of God himself and his grace. There is much else too. Prayer is a means by which we can confess[4], feel forgiveness[5], gain strength[6] and remember the needs of others.[7] We can also discover a security in life that gives an underlying peace[8] – and a reassuring awareness of an eternal dimension to our ongoing relationship with a loving God.

We were made for prayer. It is a natural part of being human.

FACE THE FACTS

* If prayer – talking with God – can be seen as a normal and natural part of relationship, why are some people so reluctant to embrace it?
* What kind of things might prayer be able to help us with, or do for us?

IT BRINGS DEPTH OF SECURITY

Relationship with God – having faith in his constant care – brings a depth of security and purpose to life, with all its twists and turns, that can't be found to the same extent anywhere else. It doesn't excuse us from unwelcome challenges or even tragedies – Jesus never promised us a trouble-free life – but the strength of this relationship can be our mainstay, and help us get other relationships right and in better perspective.

SOME PEOPLE THINK Christians use their 'religion' as a crutch – that they are basically weak people who need special or imaginary support. It doesn't seem to occur to them that Christians come from all walks of life, have a wide variety of strengths, weaknesses and interests, and carry out some of the most arduous tasks imaginable. There is a place and role for everyone – some dramatic and demanding, others mundane and unheralded. But the assumption that Christians are weak fails to note that Jesus himself not only chose and embraced suffering to an unthinkable degree, but also told his followers they would face hardships specifically *because* of their loyalty to him.[1]

Jesus never promised Christians a trouble-free life.[2] He asked for genuine commitment, personal dedication and a willingness to put 'self' last. What he *did* promise was that he would always be with us[3], ready to guide, support and strengthen. He taught that when we bind ourselves fully to him, we find inner peace and rest that cannot be found elsewhere[4] – and he does indeed provide reassurance in challenging times.

To choose Christianity in the hope of having an easy, trouble-free life would be a mistake. Those who expect 'favours' and constant happiness are not only disappointed but also miss out on what true relationship is. It isn't one-sided. Jesus gives us the dignity – and challenge – of making our contribution to his world and his purposes for it.[5]

Those who ensure that they hang on to self-centred ambition or personal happiness at all costs are, ironically, eventually seen to be avoiding the deeper obligations of humanity – love for God and others. In their desire to appear self-made and self-sufficient, they forget than none of us can be either of these. We all depend, and have already depended on, the input of others for whatever success or progress we have made. Those who accept their need of each other and dependence on God, ultimately have the joy of finding it liberating. It helps each of us get our own life and importance in perspective. It gives us reasons for living that go beyond our own little world or interests.

Open, honest relationship with God teaches us much about ourselves.[6] That is why so many people avoid it – and it is why many others are glad they didn't.

FACE THE FACTS
* Compare the suggestion that some people may view Christianity as a 'crutch', with Jesus' warnings to his followers that they could face hardship because they follow him.
* What makes us feel secure?
* What is the security that is found in Jesus?

Jesus' teaching that we should love our enemies and do good to those who hate us isn't easy to put into practice. He summed things up by saying, 'So in everything, do to others what you would have them do to you'. Pure and simple.

'**THE ONLY THING** we learn from history is that we learn nothing from history.' This gem of wisdom is attributed to Georg Wilhelm Friedrich Hegel, but he isn't the only person to have voiced these sentiments. We merely have to observe the mistakes of yesterday being made today to realise we haven't learned much. When the Hebrew nation was establishing itself, there wasn't a great deal of civilised history to fall back on. A glance at the early books of the Old Testament shows there were some ugly primitive practices taking place. Some basic laws were required to provide foundational principles for conduct and behaviour. The Ten Commandments were badly needed – and given.[1] Other laws followed, some introduced to cover specific situations of the age.

The concept of 'an eye for an eye' seems to have been introduced to promote legal equity or fairness whenever some wrong had been committed.[2] Essentially, it was a way of ensuring that retribution didn't get out of hand, or vengeance and vigilantes take over. The laws also included 'life for life'[3] or thieves becoming slaves if they had no means of paying back what they had stolen.

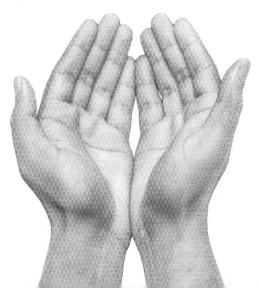

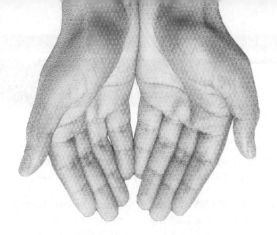

The ensuing years brought more laws and, in some cases, growing harshness. Had the nation learned much from history by the time Jesus came?

Jesus obviously felt the need to move the nation and its understanding on from 'an eye for an eye'. Living by this maxim in daily life isn't known to solve problems. It usually inflames situations and prompts more retaliation. In any case, humanity has finer qualities to call upon. Life doesn't have to be one long sequence of 'tit for tat'.

Jesus lifted people's sight to responding with love rather than with enmity. 'Love your enemies,'[4] he said. 'Bless those who curse you, do good to those who hate you, and pray for those who … persecute you' (*World English Bible*). Was this logical or possible? Jesus says 'yes' on both counts. What his hearers didn't know then was that he was soon to put his own teaching into practice. He did so as he hung on the cross and prayed, 'Father, forgive them'.[5]

Jesus doesn't advocate or choose 'an eye for an eye'. That clearly isn't his way of doing things. He offers us something better – and asks us to live by it too.

FACE THE FACTS
* In what ways did Jesus update the law of love?
* How important was it that the law should be updated – become better understood?
* How did Jesus show that 'an eye for an eye' is not how he deals with us? What are the implications for how we treat each other?

Jesus – Son of God – said he had come to serve. He frequently reminded his disciples that to put serving others before their own needs and importance was the way to true greatness.

THE DISCIPLES DIDN'T like Jesus telling them that he was a servant. 'I am among you as one who serves,'[1] he said. It was a concept that didn't sit easily with them and which they found difficult to grasp. In fairness, not many people thought in these terms for the Almighty. A god is for ruling and being obeyed. How can God be God and yet serve? Jesus not only managed it, but showed how even the 'greatest' among us can be servants – that greatness is actually found, and best expressed, in serving.[2]

The Gospels reveal that the disciples were constantly quibbling about who was the greatest. Even on the evening of Jesus' crucifixion, when other matters should have claimed their attention – they still quarrelled about greatness.[3] That was when Jesus, with one last dramatic lesson, washed their feet and left a symbol of servanthood that is still with us today.[4]

Serving his creation isn't a contradictory concept for God. Relationship with him allows for interaction, giving and receiving. Without these concepts relationship is dead. In the same way that parents can serve the needs of their children and remain the figurehead, so God has no difficulty in meeting our needs and remaining in control.[5] In fact, as we ask him to meet them we realise all the more how much we need him.[6]

The word 'servant' has different implications in different cultures, though all ultimately include serving someone else. As a man, Jesus knew how to obey his Father and to carry through his will.[7] In doing so, he was serving us – restoring our relationship with God in ways which are beyond our wit or capabilities. Yet it would be wrong to think of God serving us in Jesus only for the short period when he was on earth. Serving is in God's heart and nature.[8] His care for his creation was both emphasised by Jesus while he was on earth and seen in the priorities of his life. He is still there for us today.

Jesus' authority is not diminished by his servanthood. It is heightened whenever we come to him with our varied needs, and find we are served in love[9] – discovering a wholeness, a completeness, that can't be found anywhere else. The apostle Paul tells us to 'serve one another humbly in love'.[10] There is no better way to live.

FACE THE FACTS

* The disciples found it difficult to grasp that God, in the person of Jesus, had come to serve them, even though he gave great emphasis to it. How well do you embrace the concept?
* What does the word 'servant' imply in your culture?
* Why is service a mark of greatness?

HOW NOT TO MISS THE BEST

Jesus said that if we want to find life's best we can do so by centring on the joy of giving. He also said that the surest way to miss out on life's best is to look after your own interests only.

SELF-PRESERVATION IS a natural instinct. It makes sense to look after ourselves and ensure our basic needs are met. We have an obvious responsibility to ourselves to take care of the life we have been given. But consistently prioritising our own interests? That is a different matter.

Naturally, we need to recognise that not everyone is confident or strong enough to be always thinking of the needs of others. Some have heavy burdens or deep problems that mean it is beyond them. They deserve our understanding when they seem preoccupied with their own concerns. They merit our care as well – and sometimes we are in their number.

Most people seem to have a reasonably balanced approach to giving and receiving, helping others and being helped – nothing out of the ordinary, just normal, useful behaviour. So what did Jesus mean when he said that those who make 'saving' their life their priority will 'lose' it – and those who 'lose' their life for him and his purposes will 'save' it?[1] The language could seem extreme.

Jesus was inviting us to think beyond the ordinary, beyond playing safe. He was pointing to a better way, issuing a challenge that

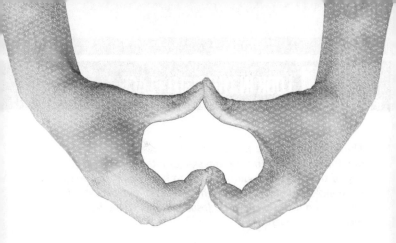

could be life-changing, but costly. What are our priorities? What matters most to us – our own comfort or something beyond self? A better lifestyle or a better world? A bit of each? And what about underlying motives and intentions? And basic attitude – do we give without counting the cost, or always ask 'what do I get out of it?' Not all of us have discovered – as Francis of Assisi did – that 'It is more blessed to give than to receive'.[2]

Jesus was promising his hearers that by inviting God into the centre of their life, they would be enriched – immeasurably. He was letting them know that if they dared to follow him and embrace his good, eternal purposes, they would find fullness of life – life's best.[3] But they would only find out by doing it. It is the same for us.

On the other hand, we are free to carry on as if we haven't heard him. Protect our own interests, play it safe, keep Jesus at a distance – lose out. Our choices have their consequences.

We only live once. Life's best, or a 'safe' existence? It's our call.

FACE THE FACTS

* How does putting our own interests first hinder our finding life's best?
* How might inviting Jesus into the centre of your life change your priorities? Would you welcome the changes?
* What might Jesus mean by fullness of life?

The way to life is not found in human power bases, force, manipulation or even supreme skill or intelligence. It is found in and through love – but we need to have our eyes open to its possibilities and look in the right place. Whereas science helps us understand how things work, Jesus takes us to the heart of life's meaning and purpose.

'**TWO MEN LOOKED** through prison bars, one saw mud the other saw stars.' It's a fact of life that we each see things differently. Some of us are optimistic, others pessimistic. Some look for the best, others for the worst. Part of the reason why we see things from different perspectives is our conditioning – the way we were brought up. Various influences, from parents and teachers, to friends and bosses, have their effect on the way we think and act. They each have a bearing, to a greater or lesser degree, on how we decide on life's values.

The values we live by can be the difference between finding Christian faith and hardly noticing it at all. Jesus once spoke about the 'wise and learned' missing out and 'little children' finding the best.[1] It isn't difficult to see why.

If our day-to-day values automatically count God out of every equation, we are unlikely to realise our need of him. When our priorities are centred on our preferences or wants, other issues won't be our natural concern. A person fixed on making money, seeing time as money, rating status above relationships, or even

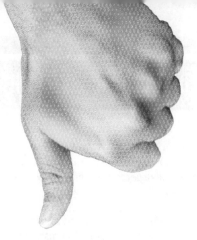

focusing on close family to the exclusion of wider obligations, can't be expected to be drawn to the values of Jesus.[2] It's unlikely to happen, until or unless something dramatic occurs to force a change of approach. The necessary openness, and the humility that comes from being aware of personal shortcomings, are crowded out. Such references may even be resented if mentioned.

Life's values can't be found in science, either. Science gives us information through which we develop expertise in the building blocks of life – but it doesn't and cannot answer the needs of the spirit. Discoveries through scientific research and experiment open doors to all kinds of possibilities – both good and bad. They provide the potential for unimagined progress and also for self-destruction. We have good cause to thank God for science, and the astounding development it produces, but we must look elsewhere for values and meaning. Life has many dimensions.

Jesus says life's values and meaning are found in relationship – especially open, honest relationship with a God who gives and advocates love.[3] Human power bases, skills, intelligence and politics, all have their place. But they can never be adequate substitutes for the main reason we were born – relationship with God.

FACE THE FACTS
* How were your life values shaped? Who played a significant part in the shaping?
* How high has relationship with God been in your priorities?
* What is the point of relationship with God?

Jesus lived by what he taught. What he preached, he lived out with a consistency that no other teacher has come anywhere near to emulating. When all aspects of his life are examined or scrutinised, they hold together.

JESUS, SON OF God, didn't become involved in setting individual rules for every little circumstance in life. Instead, he gave us the over-arching rule of love, on which we can base all our dealings. So we need to remind ourselves that the love of which Jesus spoke was not simply the 'warm feeling' kind, but involves loyalty, honesty, faithfulness, commitment, giving and forgiving – and that it can be costly.

Jesus was wonderfully compassionate towards those who had made a mess of their lives. It didn't matter to him whether they were rich or poor, male or female, Jew or non-Jew.[1] If they turned to him he was ready to meet their need. He embraced people of both high and low reputation. From ruler of the synagogue[2] to prostitute[3], he gave them his individual attention. He still does.

The care he gave and the interest he showed often brought criticism. He made himself unpopular by standing with those who needed him most, even if they may not have deserved his support in the eyes of others.[4] The love he showed also involved the sternness of discipline, and promoting what was right when others may have preferred easier ways.[5] Neither did he omit to point out

that injustices and refusal to forgive others have their ultimate consequences.[6]

His maxim 'Do to others what you would have them do to you' was simple and straightforward.[7] His teaching didn't give preference to one class above another, or allocate grades of wrongdoing. The love of Christ reached all who wanted it – and he gave it with honesty, truth and a commitment to restore as required. Those who didn't want it were free to reject it – and free to reject the concept of 'doing to others what you would have them do to you'.

Yet his patience with people who let him down[8] and his belief in the goodness of those who showed little signs of it[9], led to lives being transformed from bad to good, from hopelessness to fulfilment.

There are times when to love is not the attractive option, holding little hope of success or appreciation. Jesus didn't hide this from his followers and he doesn't hide it from us. He didn't compromise his love for us. He embraced love's challenges and gave himself to us supremely.

He lived and died what he taught. Jesus adds up.

FACE THE FACTS

* What does Jesus' care for the disadvantaged and despised – often to the cost of his own popularity – say about the nature of God?
* Why would he have been criticised for it?
* Examine the consistency of his life with its foundation on love.

When things turned ugly and Jesus was misrepresented, defamed, abused, arrested and condemned to death, everything he had taught about selflessness, surrender, giving and forgiving was confirmed in his responses. He especially prayed for the forgiveness of those who killed him.

HIGHLIGHTING THE AUTHENTICITY of Jesus' life, its clear integrity and purity of purpose, isn't difficult. His teaching, relationships and responses were seamless in their expression of love and are further enhanced by the evidence of what happens when we act on his words and example. There is, quite simply, no better way to live, no more effective code to put into action, and no one else to follow who merits our total allegiance.[1] His life spoke for itself then and it does so today.

Thinking through what it cost him is another matter. Having given time and effort to teaching the way of love with clarity, Jesus found himself and his words being deliberately misrepresented.[2] His work was undermined.[3] He faced jealousy disguised as righteousness – with those who should have known better, trying to catch him out with trick questions.[4] He was more than equal to them, yet all the time he was working in a climate of growing hostility from 'officialdom'. He was accused of breaking (his own) laws[5], being too friendly with people who most needed his care[6] and, ultimately, condemned for telling the truth about who he was.[7]

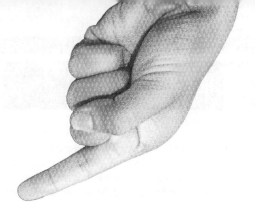

As all this (and more) took place, Jesus would have been aware that simple people were being led astray, damaged by the lies of their leaders. As the authorities resorted to political power and force to arrest him, his message of love, servanthood and forgiveness looked neither attractive nor workable. When he was tried, condemned and crucified, all that he stood for looked discredited. Even his disciples, those whom he had trained for three years, ran away[8] – in spite of the warnings and preparation he had given them. Had they heard and learned nothing?

Jesus didn't panic. He didn't react with anger or threaten retribution. He put into practice what he had been teaching, still putting other people's needs before his own. His prayer from the cross, 'Father, forgive them, for they do not know what they are doing'[9], stands as a supreme reminder of an unshakeable, ongoing care.

Jesus withstood all that was thrown at him, because he had full confidence in who he was[10] – and the power of divine love within him. He knew what *he* was doing. Through his death would come Resurrection – and our salvation.[11]

FACE THE FACTS

* Jesus highlighted the place of forgiveness through his teaching and example. How might this impact your relationship with him – and others?
* In spite of being misrepresented, undermined, abandoned, abused and condemned to death, Jesus never lost confidence in the supremacy of love. Why?

Questions about suffering – why does it exist and why doesn't God prevent it? – have always tested the human spirit. Jesus chose to suffer. In making the deliberate choice to identify fully with us, God's Son embraced suffering, and did so to a degree we can hardly imagine.

IT ISN'T UNUSUAL for someone to want to take the place of a loved one who is suffering. Something noble in the human spirit prompts such responses and we understand why they occur. They are an expression of love that can be costly.

Jesus chose to suffer.[1] His coming to earth wasn't a chance happening. It wasn't random. It was planned.[2] Jesus would come. He would become vulnerable, open to the limitations and hindrances of humanity. He would identify with and live for his creation[3] – and, in so doing, he would suffer. As with all humans, he would die.

By choosing to be like us, Jesus was embracing suffering at our level. God would experience for himself – as a human – hunger,[4] thirst,[5] homelessness,[6] tiredness,[7] bereavement[8] and physical pain.[9] He would also be exposed to danger, hostility, rejection and people working against him. All this was his decision – he made himself vulnerable.

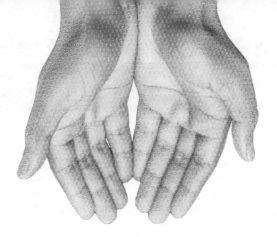

It may be easy for cynics to dismiss this as a sham, but the evidence shows otherwise. Jesus refused to use special powers for himself, such as turning stones into bread[10], and wept openly over the sins of Jerusalem[11] and the death of a friend.[12] In particular, as he faced the horrors of torture and crucifixion, Jesus prayed that God his Father would grant him a way to avoid them. In the Garden of Gethsemane he prayed, 'Father, if you are willing, take this cup from me.'[13] He didn't want to face the pain, the suffering, the total humiliation. Contemplating the agony of going through with it was overwhelming. Luke's Gospel tells us his sweat was like great drops of blood falling to the ground.[14] This was real. He chose to suffer, but he didn't *want* to suffer.

Fortunately for us, there was more to his prayer. It revealed his resolve and concluded, 'yet not my will, but yours be done.' Jesus went through with it – abandoned by his followers, hated by religious leaders, despised by those who felt let down and jeered by mocking crowds.[15]

Why did he do it? He had seen our pain – the pain of alienation from God, the pain of our helplessness in putting things right, the suffering of missing out on what we were meant to be. He wanted us to be relieved of that pain, to make us whole again – and suffered for us.[16]

FACE THE FACTS
*Why did Jesus choose to suffer?
*Take time to consider the reality of all he endured in his suffering.
* In what ways might the suffering of Jesus, Son of God, help us today?

If ever we are tempted to blame God for everything that is or goes wrong, Jesus' suffering and death show that he freely took all we humans could throw at him. The depths and horrors of the pain he experienced left him feeling alienated from God the Father. He actually said so. Jesus understands suffering and its effects.

ANY SURVEY THAT asks non-believers why they don't believe in God, will find 'suffering' at the top of the list of answers. It isn't surprising that those who watch loved ones suffer, or who have had more than their fair share of pain, have questions to put to the Almighty – especially a God of love – if he exists. And why do 'bad' things happen to 'good' people?[1]

Sometimes, of course, we make our own pain or are the cause of suffering for others. Our thoughtless or reckless behaviour has consequences. We know where the blame lies if even we don't readily admit it. But this doesn't explain why the innocent so often suffer, or why natural disasters wreak havoc and misery. Insurance companies call them 'acts of God'. Should he accept the blame?

It isn't just a case of wanting to blame someone. Those who question are often genuinely bewildered, deeply hurt and feel justifiably let down. Their questions merit full consideration – but who can speak for God?[2]

There is no doubt that pain is at the centre of life. It plays a crucial – even irreplaceable – role in human development and progress.

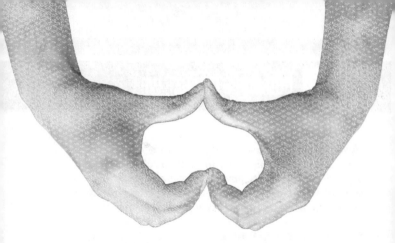

We look at the cost in time and effort on so much of what we achieve and say 'No pain, no gain'. We even find satisfaction in counting the cost of our efforts and accept the suffering as a healthy part of life – though not in every case. The fact is, suffering will always play a part – welcome and unwelcome – in making us who we are.

If we decide after due consideration, or simply in the midst of painful suffering, that God is to blame for allowing the world to be as it is, we don't find him hiding. We find Jesus on the cross taking all humankind's wrongdoing on his suffering shoulders.[3] Every bit of blame we wish to throw at him – including our own – he took. The apostle Paul described Jesus as 'becoming sin' for us.[4] The weight of it left him feeling totally alienated from God and he said so.[5] We can only try to imagine the depths of this experience, embraced for us.

His identification with us and our suffering was total. And by relieving us of our guilt, an unparalleled good thing happened to 'bad people'. Jesus made it possible for us to be right with God.

FACE THE FACTS

* Consider the integral part pain plays in our life. What value might it have? What are the negatives?
* For what kind of things might you want to blame God?
* For what kind of things could God justifiably blame us?

Having given us free will, God accepts the consequences. Without our free will we would be no more than robots or puppets. With free will we can create havoc. We can also grow, learn, develop and discover things that cannot be understood by any other means. We are also free to ask for his guidance.

LIFE WITHOUT FREE will would be pointless. Imagine every day with no control over our own decisions and actions. We would feel helpless, stripped of dignity, and either boil over with frustration or simply not have the capacity to think things through. What would be the point – of anything?

Thankfully, human beings have the capacity to reason, argue, choose, change their mind, develop, receive love, respond, form values and engage in relationships at different levels. We are unique and obviously have a higher place – and responsibility – in creation.[1]

Free will is at the heart of what makes us who we are. It is at the centre of all our relationships and provides us with some leading clues as to where we might find meaning and fulfilment, both as individuals and collectively. It points to the natural logic in Christian belief that relationship with God is the most important one of all. Having created us 'in his image'[2] – and therefore with the capacity to relate to him – it isn't surprising that God has given us the privilege of relationship with him. Rather than hide in heavenly splendour that we can only vainly imagine, he came to us

as a man in Jesus – and left us teaching and example that we can relate to and understand.

For any relationship to be real, we need to be able to make personal choices, and this naturally applies to our relationship to God as well as to one another. As we use our free will we can bring great comfort, support and blessing. We can also be harsh, unthinking, cruel and create havoc, both for ourselves and for others – often those closest to us.

It isn't surprising that we sometimes wish God would forcefully 'intervene' and prevent atrocities or unwelcome incidents.[3] We may even complain that he is not using his power, yet any forced intervention would involve God restricting our free will. Would we really want to be controlled? If so, it would mean God taking away what he gifted us – the freedom to become the individuals we are.

Through relationship with him we are able to ask God for guidance for our own actions, and strength and wisdom when we are on the receiving end of the abuse of free will by others. As always, we have the choice to accept or ignore. That's free will.

FACE THE FACTS
* Why is free will essential to life – and relationships?
* Why do you think God gave us free will?
* Try to assess how well you use it.

Whenever we choose to hurt others, bring pain upon ourselves, or ignore what he has planned for us, God still suffers. It matters to him. He doesn't take back our free will or restrain us from using it. He does, however, wait to guide and support us if we will give him the time.

WE EARLIER TOOK a look at God in Christ suffering. We saw that his suffering took various forms, and ended with his death on a cross. And it could be possible to conclude that God chose to suffer only for the brief period he was on earth in Jesus – to save us – and didn't suffer before he came or since. The Almighty suffering is not a concept that usually comes easily to us.

So it might help to briefly re-examine our concept of God and ask why he came to earth in Jesus. Was it to 'pull everyone into line'? That isn't how Jesus described it. He said something quite different – that he had come to 'seek and save the lost'.[1] He told the parable of the lost sheep, highlighting the shepherd 'rejoicing' when he found it.[2] We are meant to understand ourselves to be the sheep and God the shepherd. God is overjoyed at our returning to the fold. His joy replaces his pain. Jesus came to earth because God cared.

In the Old Testament, amid references to how God may deal with those who disobey him, are glimpses of him mourning the rejection of his people[3], and his loving plans for them.[4] He had

seen their self-inflicted suffering, and it pained him. He had in mind to rescue them. God's heart is to forgive. He did not give up. Jesus came.

God's identification with our suffering, seen in the life of Jesus, didn't end when he ceased to live among us as a man. Jesus promised he would send his Spirit to be with us[5] – and that he would remain with us 'to the very end of the age'.[6] He would come as our guide and comforter[7], to help us discern truth, to be our companion. Today, God is at work in his world, in and among his people – at the heart of life – recognised and enjoyed by those who welcome him.

Earlier, we noted that suffering is a barrier to some people believing in God. The reverse is also the case. 'Suffering' is at the top of many believer's reasons for having their faith in God confirmed. In their darkest days they have known his presence, comfort and healing in a more powerful way than ever before. As he suffers with us, he has his own way of bringing healing – for this life and the next.[8]

FACE THE FACTS

* What does Jesus coming to 'seek and save the lost' tell us about the heart of God?
* How might our suffering – or difficulties in watching a loved one suffer – bring us into greater depth of relationship with God?

Libraries of books have been written on this subject. Put simply, its purpose was to bring man and God together – to help us see both our need of him and his overwhelming love for us. He said he had come to 'seek and save' the lost – and he did.

THERE ARE MANY ways in which the purpose of Jesus' death can be understood. Its impact was, has been, and is immense – in truth, more far-reaching than we can realise or fully know. People of all cultures, learning and walks of life have struggled to find the right words for the past 2,000 years. There is so much to say and so much to put into perspective.

The fact is, its effect touches every area of life and is ongoing. All the world's issues met at Calvary when Jesus was crucified there.[1] The enormity of what was happening couldn't be seen, yet everything that has ever mattered was being addressed. It happened as we tried to destroy God.

So who or what met at Calvary? People met at Calvary – men, women, priests, rulers, soldiers, criminals, mockers, bystanders.[2] They were there with their opinions and emotions – missing the point and not able to see what was really happening. On this Jerusalem hillside, beyond their comprehension, evil met goodness, lies met truth, despair met hope, hate met love, doubt met faith and death met life – in the man who was God.

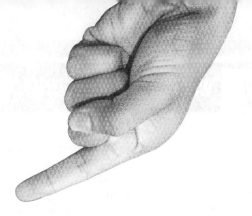

Jesus had come to put right what was wrong between humanity and God. He came to do for us what we couldn't do for ourselves. He described it as to seek and save us. When we examine our relationship with God – or lack of it – we see that God wants it to develop more than we do. His loving purposes for us go deeper than we imagine or seem to care. His readiness to forgive – even those things for which we feel unable to forgive ourselves – is constantly conspicuous throughout the Gospels.[3] He meant it and showed he meant it.

In order to save us, God in man defeated evil with goodness, hatred with love, and brought life out of his death. At Calvary, humanity was seen in its worst light – trying to destroy God. By not resisting[4], Jesus helped us see ourselves as we really are – standing in great need of him and his goodness.

God was seen in his true light too – loving, forgiving, restoring and renewing. Jesus' subsequent Resurrection also revealed God as all-powerful, all-conquering and offering us new life. The purpose of Jesus' death was to reconcile us to God.[5] He smashed the barriers. What happens next is up to us.

FACE THE FACTS
* The actions of Jesus indicate that God wants us to have relationship with him more than we do. Why does he bother?
* What does Jesus' violent death say about humanity and what does it say about God?

On a personal note, it will make as much difference as each of us wants it to make. To accept our need of Jesus and his goodness, and to commit ourselves to his will and way, involves a measure of humility – not always our best feature – yet it opens the door for what Jesus called 'fullness of life'. Relationship with Almighty God can be viewed as the privilege of all privileges.

JESUS ACHIEVED GOD'S great purpose of reconciling humanity to God. Whatever was preventing our being able to enjoy unimpaired relationship with him, has been removed. Jesus smashed the barriers. Mission accomplished! Yet the benefits of this reconciliation aren't universally experienced. Might that seem strange, after such an almighty effort from God to put things right?

The answer isn't complicated. It takes two to effect a reconciliation, to make it work. God has given us free will, he has given us the dignity of choice. For relationship and reconciliation to have any meaning of worth, it must be two-way. We can ignore the barriers being down if we choose to do so. We can keep God at arm's length, decide to ignore him, or even conclude that he doesn't exist without ever daring to test our theory. There is something within us that doesn't want to face the truth about ourselves. It may be too revealing, too painful. Any move towards an open, honest, all-embracing God might mean that we have to take our barriers down too.

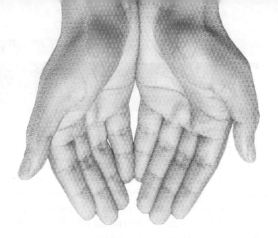

What might our barriers be? Within our personal list we may find pride, stubbornness, or a refusal to admit any deficiency, or that we could become a better person with God's help. There is fear of the unknown, what it might cost or lead to – or perhaps fear of the difference it might make to us. Other barriers might simply be our reluctance to believe that God is that interested in us, or we have an overwhelming sense of unworthiness. We are a mixed bunch, no two of us the same. We each have our own issues to face – or ignore.

To do the opposite and move towards God, opens up a new world. We find acceptance, and a relationship in which we are able not only to be completely open, but also in which it is *best* to be open. Trying to hide our faults from God is like trying to hide our pain from our doctor – foolish.

Discovering God as a lifelong companion brings transformation at many levels. The experience is different for each of us. We all start from a different place – intellectually, culturally, age-wise and through the effects of life experience. Relationship with God is the privilege of all privileges.[1] And God wants us to make the most of it.[2]

FACE THE FACTS

* What barriers might we put up to keep God at bay?
* Is there any reason why you wouldn't welcome the privilege of honest, open relationship with God?
* If so, what do you think Jesus might say about it?

HIS DEATH WASN'T THE END

When Jesus died on the cross it looked as if evil had defeated goodness. The man who preached love was dead. The people who had lied about him, used their power to condemn him and then arranged his torture and killing, seemed to have won. But Jesus was aware that love's power was stronger than evil, stronger than death. Jesus – love personified – couldn't be contained. He rose from the dead. His Resurrection stands supreme in human history.

THERE IS NO shortage of examples where evil seems to defeat goodness.[1] They occur every day. 'Bad' people trick 'good' people on a regular basis – because it seems to pay off. Innocent or gullible victims fall foul of scheming manipulators. Some lose their life savings, others are just made to look stupid. Far too many never recover to become the person they were before being damaged by the callous actions of others. They live with the consequences every day.

The situation didn't look good on the night of the crucifixion. Judged at face value, all that Jesus had preached and stood for looked exposed as idealistic nonsense. His fine words about love and the heavenly Father's care had seemingly come to nothing.[2] Evil people are more forceful, they get their own way – and 'get away' with murder. That's how it looked – and that's how we often look at things too.

Time would soon tell that this view was entirely wrong. In retrospect, it was the wicked who were exposed for their shameful, conniving, ruthless actions, while the unrelenting power

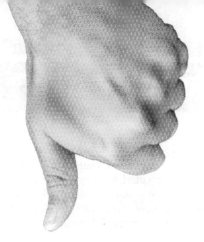

of the love of God was revealed to be stronger than all the forces of evil. Ultimately, divine love creates good out of all that is worst. To be precise, God – the source of life and love – is almighty.[3] It cannot be any other way with God.

Jesus isn't the only one who has died in what have seemed to be tragic circumstances, with injustice dominating the scene. In the years since his death, evil has at times seemed to laugh in the face of all that is good, as murders, rapes, flawed judgements, incapacity and slavery have ended people's lives in seeming humiliation or disgrace. Welcome and unwelcome experiences are not shared out equally. Life is 'not fair'. Jesus obviously knew this[4], and we do, too. But life needs to make sense – especially life that comes from a loving, creator God.

The Resurrection of Jesus changed everything. His life and death were now viewed from an eternal perspective. Ours can be too. Through the Resurrection our lives also have eternal perspective. Death is not the end. Human judgement and circumstances will be superseded. Wrongs will be righted. Joy will replace pain[5] – and the justice and mercy of God will reign supreme.[6]

FACE THE FACTS

* Why does the Resurrection stand supreme in human history?
* Consider its implications regarding the power of good and evil.
* Consider its implications for your life within the loving purposes of God.
* What eternal perspective does it bring to any of earth's unfinished business – rights and wrongs?

It didn't take long for those who had followed Jesus to realise that the divine power at work in his Resurrection could give new life to us too. Evil had been defeated, bringing release from our failures, with freedom to start again – and with God's help. God has always had our best interests at heart. Jesus' life, teaching, suffering, death and (now) Resurrection give compelling evidence to this.

SOME FIND IT hard to believe that God has our best interests at heart. They see him as severe and uncompromising – even 'eye for an eye' with his justice. That's not what we see in Jesus. His coming to earth *in itself* indicates a God who loves us more than we seem able to grasp.[1]

And why *wouldn't* our Creator want us to find the best in life? Would he really create the human race simply so that he would feel important, only to be worshipped and obeyed? Where is the satisfaction in a motive so controlling – so limiting in outcomes?

It is, of course, essential that we have a sense of reverence, awe and wonder towards God.[2] Without them we are bereft. We would (and often do) think too highly of ourselves.[3] Respect for God gives us focus and accountability – and it also provides the foundation for exploring the loving purposes he has for us. Within those loving purposes is our free will to choose to love him in return.

Jesus' life of love and sacrifice in death is a clear statement of God's intention for us to 'get the message'. Almighty God – God in

Christ – died for us. And the Resurrection opened the way to new life, new beginnings and the fullness of relationship with him.[4]

Hesitancy may come from us in a number of ways. Lack of interest, tiredness, feeling that we already have all we need or want. Reluctance to admit our need of God's forgiveness. Assuming we aren't worthy of forgiveness. Not wanting to be subject to anyone. Wanting to hold on to what may not be wise.

Whatever the case, without some moment when we are conscious of submitting ourselves to God in humility, we have no defining point for our commitment or a new beginning.[5] There will have been no moment when we open our heart to God and acknowledge his supremacy in our life. Without accepting his supremacy there is no point.[6] Either we want God to be God to us – with all that involves – or we don't. There is no 'in between' position that makes sense. The conditions are the same for us all.

When we respond to his 'follow me' we discover the new life he planned for us. It is our own. No one else's.[7] The one where we find ourselves. The one he has always promised we would find.

FACE THE FACTS

* Consider how each of us is the reason for Jesus' life, death and Resurrection.
* Consider the appropriateness of a personal response.
* 'Without some moment when we are conscious of submitting ourselves to God in humility, we have no defining point for our commitment or a new beginning.' Why is humility before God vital to a right relationship with him?

The transformation in the first disciples was remarkable. They were their own best evidence for what the power of God does. The Church grew from their witness. For the past 2,000 years, countless people have discovered for themselves ways in which God transforms lives at every level.

AUTHENTICITY SHINES THROUGH when you are your own best evidence for what you are promoting or teaching. In the disciples' case, their transformation was so remarkable that thousands were immediately convinced of their message. Their post-Resurrection meetings with Jesus[1] had changed their fearful, introspective confusion into something altogether different. Their openness to being guided by the Spirit of God released inner resources they didn't know they could possess. They became assured, out-going and confident – people who changed the course of the world.[2]

The change in them was dramatic. It needed to be. Things had moved fast in just a few weeks – from Jesus preaching in Jerusalem to his arrest, trial and death, and then to the Resurrection and a world of new possibilities. Yet they were still the same people. John was still John, Peter was still Peter and so on – but they were now becoming the people Jesus had always known they could become.

The word 'transformation' implies something dramatic. It speaks of 'before' and 'after' and the difference. People who have turned to Jesus through the centuries use the word because it genuinely

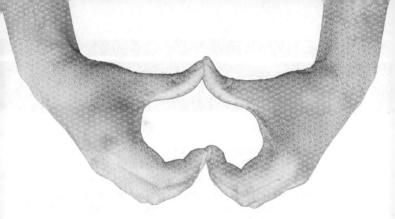

applies to their life. Changes can be sudden – even sensational. And the transformations – from depravity to dedication, bullying to benevolence, tyranny to tenderness – are always their own best evidence of God's transforming power in a person's life.

But transformation doesn't necessarily occur all at once. And we are all changing every day. We can't avoid it. When we consider the dramatic changes needed in some cases – to unlearn a lifetime of corruption, deceit and unthinking self-interest, for instance – time is required for the transformation to be carried through. This is why the apostle Paul speaks of our 'being transformed'[3] – an ongoing process. Fully understanding what is involved in being a Christian doesn't happen overnight.

Transformation in Christian terms doesn't mean we become somebody else. We are still the same person – the one God has loved all the time, even in our most shameful, hidden moments. He has never given up on us. Yet, as we allow ourselves to be guided by him, we also grow more like him – in love, joy, peace, patience, kindness, goodness, faithfulness, gentleness and self-control.[4] When Paul wrote of our being transformed it was more and more into the likeness of Jesus himself.

FACE THE FACTS

* How useful is the evidence of transformed lives – before and after – in helping us see what God can do for those who ask him?
* However suddenly or gradually transformation may take place, each of us must first make our own decision to place ourselves in God's good hands. How ready are you to let God guide you through life?

31 JESUS DOESN'T FORCE US

If relationship means anything it has to be genuine. Even though Jesus' demonstration of love was supremely costly, there is no question of God forcing anyone to accept the love he offers. As the Gospel records show, Jesus – the founder of Christianity – rejected utterly the use of force or violence to promote his purposes. He still does. Such force would be contrary to all he is and stands for. It would be counter-productive – and meaningless too.

ONE OF THE defining marks of Christianity is that its founder, Jesus Christ, never used or advocated force to gain converts. He waged no battles, fought no wars[1] and rejected any suggestion that he had come to lead a revolt against Roman occupation of Jerusalem.[2] In this way, he left a clear message for his followers – do not use force or violence to spread Christianity. To do so would be to betray everything for which he stands. In the volatile climate of the 21st century, it is important that his message is heard – loud and clear. Other generations give evidence of the chaos caused by those who ignored it.

As the architect of relationships, God knows that to force people into submission, or to do what you demand, destroys relationships. The trust and mutual respect on which they are built become damaged. Forcing someone to love you is as impossible as it is foolish. It is not part of God's way with us or his plans for us. Had he wanted to use force to make us turn to him, Jesus would not have arrived as a helpless baby.[3] A baby – dependent and vulnerable – needs love, invites love. This is how the majesty of

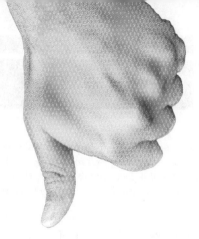

God revealed itself.[4] This was splendour beyond our reckoning – and still beyond our understanding.[5]

And so to us. Most of us will at some time have been frustrated by the reluctance of loved ones to be helped or advised. We have seen them reject kindness and make unnecessary, even life-damaging, mistakes. But to step in with force does not win over hearts. It breeds resentment.

We are told that Jesus wept over Jerusalem. He could see what the people were failing to see, and wept for them.[6] But to force them to see what already stared them in the face? This would make a mockery of free will. It isn't how God deals with us.

Jesus will never force us to follow and we need to learn the lesson from him. Frustrated as we may be with our friends, family and acquaintances who are missing out on life's best, or seem to be making unwise choices, we still need to allow them the dignity of choosing their own path. We must also learn how to be there for them, if and when they turn to us. Just as Jesus is.

FACE THE FACTS

* Using force in any relationship is always a defeat. Take time to think through the implications of Jesus not only never engaging in physical battle to 'win the world', but also never forcing people to accept what he has lovingly planned for them.
* He awaits our free will response to him. It is how he does things. You are *invited* to make your response.

Jesus was never recorded trying to persuade or cajole people into following him. When a young rich man rejected his terms and walked away from him, Jesus didn't plead with him. He let him go. It is still the same. He gave him the dignity of choice. He gives it to us too.

EVERY DAY WE make choices. They run through everything we do – from deciding on food, clothes and friends, to work and career. Our capacity to choose and the choices we make determine, to a large extent, how our life unfolds. Choices make an impact. In some cases, a lasting impact. Yet not everyone has the same range of choices. The country, society or family into which we are born may present us with so many options that we don't know where to start, while others have limiting restrictions imposed because of perceived lack of status or rights.

For some people, religion isn't a choice. They are born into it and if they choose to break away, it is at the risk of death. This is not so with Jesus. He invites us to choose.[1] He wants us to choose him – and so embrace fullness of life, love, freedom and the obedience to God that gives us our standard for living.

Choices say a lot about us. They reveal our preferences. They show our passion – or lack of it. Are we outgoing, studious, sporty, music-loving, self-centred, impetuous, generous, status conscious?

Our choices give the answers. We are enriched by the privilege of choice. It can be something more for which to thank God. Jesus made his choices. They were for us.[2] They weren't half-hearted, resentful or inconsistent. His choices for us were gracious, costly, all-embracing and with an integrity of consistency that stands supreme. His self-giving was total and is unparalleled.[3] The simple, clear fact is, Jesus wants us to find him, know him and enjoy the relationship for which we were born.

Who is this Jesus anyway? was written to present an opportunity for anyone who chooses to read it, to take an honest, open look at Jesus. Hopefully, it will also have provoked some of us into seeing ourselves better – or to become aware of how relationship with God gives direction and meaning to life. Its underlying aim has been to provide a means whereby an informed choice can be made. Yet the choice to respond to God in love, must be more than 'informed'. In order to feel the full benefit, it also has to be wholehearted – and includes an act of faith.

We have the dignity of choice. God bless and guide you in yours.

FACE THE FACTS
* Relationship with God, through Jesus, is the privilege of all privileges. Enjoy it.

SCRIPTURE REFERENCES

The Bible references provided here indicate where the information given in each chapter can be found. They relate to the *New International Version* unless otherwise stated.

1. JESUS IS A FACT – page 6
[1] John 20:30-31
[2] Matthew 24:35

2. HISTORY TELLS US ABOUT HIM – page 8
[1] John 18:28–19:16
[2] Mark 6:14
[3] Matthew 26:57
[4] Matthew 2:19
[5] Matthew 2:16
[6] Matthew 13:55
[7] Galatians 1:19
[8] John 21:25
[9] Matthew 1:25
[10] Luke 23:46
[11] Luke 24:1-6

3. THE NEW TESTAMENT GIVES DETAILS – page 10
[1] Mark 8:17-18
[2] Mark 9:33-35
[3] Mark 8:31-32
[4] Mark 14:50
[5] Luke 24:11
[6] Luke 24:25-27
[7] Mark 16:12-14
[8] John 20:28-29
[9] Acts 1:3
[10] John 3:16
[11] Acts 2:1-4
[12] Acts 4:1-21

4. IT SHOWS LIFE'S REALITIES – page 12
[1] Acts 2:44-45
[2] Acts 9:2
[3] Hebrews 12:14
[4] Acts 15:1-3, 6-30 and 36-40
[5] Galatians 6:1-5
[6] Galatians 6:10

5. JESUS DIED A YOUNG MAN – page 14
[1] John 7:43; 11:56-57
[2] Luke 5:21
[3] John 7:52
[4] John 7:32
[5] Matthew 6:5; Mark 7:9

[6] Luke 10:25-28
[7] Mark 7:5-8
[8] Luke 9:22
[9] Mark 1:35
[10] Luke 22:39-45
[11] Mark 14:35-36
[12] Luke 23:35
[13] John 15:13

6. WHO WAS HE? – page 16

[1] John 1:1-14
[2] 1 John 1:1-4
[3] Luke 1:26-38
[4] Matthew 1:18-25
[5] John 2:1-4
[6] John 19:25-27

7. HE WAS HUMAN – page 18

[1] Luke 2:52
[2] Luke 2:41-52
[3] Luke 3:22
[4] Luke 3:23

8. HE WAS GOD – page 20

[1] Mark 1:1; Philippians 1:2
[2] Galatians 1:1-3
[3] 2 Corinthians 5:19
[4] 1 John 1:1
[5] John 1:14
[6] Mark 1:43
[7] Matthew 9:12-13
[8] Matthew 2:6, 17-18
[9] Isaiah 52:13–53:11; Matthew 20:28
[10] Luke 2:4-7
[11] Zechariah 9:9; Matthew 21:1-5

9. WHEN DID HE FIRST BECOME NOTICED? – page 22

[1] John 1:29
[2] Matthew 3:13-17; Mark 1:9-13; Luke 3:21-22; John 1:32-34
[3] Matthew 3:13-15
[4] Matthew 3:16-17
[5] Matthew 3:11
[6] Matthew 3:1

10. HE TOOK TIME OUT – page 24

[1] Matthew 4:1
[2] Matthew 4:2-3
[3] Matthew 4:5-7
[4] Matthew 4:8-10
[5] Romans 15:3
[6] Luke 6:12-16

11. WHAT DID HE TEACH? – page 26
[1] Mark 1:27
[2] Mark 1:22
[3] Matthew 23:1-4
[4] Matthew 5:21-22, 27-28, 31-34, 38-39, 43-44
[5] Matthew 12:1-2
[6] Luke 10:25-26, 36
[7] Matthew 23:5-7, 25-26
[8] Luke 11:39-41
[9] Matthew 25:40

12. LOVE IS THE PRIORITY – page 28
[1] Mark 12:28-31; Deuteronomy 6:4-5; Leviticus 19:18
[2] 1 Corinthians 13
[3] 1 John 4:16
[4] 1 John 4:10

13. RELATIONSHIP IS THE KEY – page 30
[1] Mark 12:28-31
[2] John 15:14
[3] Matthew 11:28-30
[4] 2 Peter 3:18; 2 Corinthians 3:18
[5] John 13:34
[6] John 1:14
[7] Mark 1:16-17

14. PRAYER IS NORMAL – page 32
[1] Luke 11:1-2
[2] John 21:15-19
[3] Matthew 6:6-8
[4] Psalm 51:1-4
[5] Psalm 103:12
[6] Philippians 4:6
[7] Colossians 4:2-4
[8] Philippians 4:7

15. IT BRINGS DEPTH OF SECURITY – page 34
[1] Matthew 24:9
[2] John 16:33
[3] Matthew 28:20
[4] Matthew 11:28-30
[5] 1 Corinthians 3:9
[6] Psalm 139:23

16. LOVE YOUR ENEMIES – page 36
[1] Exodus 20:1-17
[2] Deuteronomy 19:21
[3] Exodus 21:23
[4] Matthew 5:44-45
[5] Luke 23:34

17. HE WAS A SERVANT – page 38

[1] Luke 22:27
[2] Matthew 18:1-4
[3] Luke 22:24
[4] John 13:2-17
[5] Psalm 103:13-14
[6] Matthew 6:7-8
[7] Philippians 2:5-8
[8] 2 Corinthians 8:9
[9] 1 John 1:8-10
[10] Galatians 5:13

18. HOW NOT TO MISS THE BEST – page 40

[1] Mark 8:34-37
[2] Acts 20:35
[3] John 10:10

19. LOOK IN THE RIGHT PLACE – page 42

[1] Matthew 11:25
[2] Matthew 6:24
[3] Matthew 7:12

20. HE LIVED WHAT HE TAUGHT – page 44

[1] Matthew 8:5-10; Luke 18:35-42; Mark 7:24-30
[2] Mark 5:22-24
[3] Luke 7:36-50
[4] John 8:1-11
[5] Matthew 5:23-24
[6] Matthew 6:14-15; Matthew 25:45-46
[7] Matthew 7:12
[8] Matthew 26:36-41
[9] Luke 19:1-10

21. HE PROVED ITS VALUE – page 46

[1] John 6:68-69; Acts 4:12
[2] John 18:30
[3] John 9:1-41
[4] Matthew 21:23-27
[5] Matthew 12:1-2
[6] Matthew 9:11
[7] Matthew 26:63-66
[8] Mark 14:50
[9] Luke 23:34
[10] John 13:3; Luke 23:46
[11] 1 Thessalonians 5:9

22. HE CHOSE TO SUFFER – page 48

[1] 2 Corinthians 8:9
[2] John 3:17
[3] John 1:10-14

[4] Matthew 4:2
[5] John 19:28
[6] Luke 9:58
[7] Mark 6:31
[8] John 11:14
[9] Mark 14:65
[10] Matthew 4:3-4
[11] Luke 19:41
[12] John 11:35
[13] Luke 22:42
[14] Luke 22:44
[15] Luke 23:35-36
[16] 1 Peter 2:24

23. HE SUFFERED FOR US – page 50
[1] Job 34:5-6
[2] Job 38:4
[3] 1 Peter 2:24
[4] 2 Corinthians 5:21
[5] Matthew 27:46

24. GOD GIVES US FREE WILL – page 52
[1] Psalm 8
[2] Genesis 1:26-27
[3] Psalm 10:1-12

25. HE STILL SUFFERS – page 54
[1] Luke 19.10
[2] Luke 15:3-7
[3] Hosea 11:1-2
[4] Hosea 14:4
[5] John 14:25-26
[6] Matthew 28:20
[7] John 15:26
[8] Isaiah 53:3-5

26. WHAT WAS THE PURPOSE OF HIS DEATH? – page 56
[1] Luke 23:33 (King James Version)
[2] Luke 23:35-36
[3] John 8:1-11
[4] Luke 22:52-54
[5] 2 Corinthians 5:18-21

27. WHAT DIFFERENCE DOES IT MAKE? – page 58
[1] John 14:21
[2] Matthew 7:7-8

28. HIS DEATH WASN'T THE END – page 60
[1] Psalm 12:8
[2] Matthew 6:8; Matthew 6:25-33

[3] Revelation 4:8-11
[4] Matthew 13:24-30
[5] Revelation 21:3-4
[6] Revelation 1:8; Hebrews 4:15-16

29. IT WAS THE BEGINNING – page 62
[1] 1 John 4:10
[2] Psalm 111:10
[3] Galatians 6:3
[4] 1 Corinthians 15:3-10
[5] John 20:28
[6] Colossians 1:15-20
[7] John 21:15-22

30. JESUS BRINGS TRANSFORMATION – page 64
[1] 1 Corinthians 15:3-9
[2] Acts 4:32-33
[3] 2 Corinthians 3:18
[4] Galatians 5:22-23

31. JESUS DOESN'T FORCE US – page 66
[1] Luke 22:47-54
[2] Mark 12:17
[3] Luke 2:4-7
[4] Titus 2:11
[5] 2 Corinthians 9:15
[6] Luke 19:41-44

32. IT'S OUR CHOICE – page 68
[1] Mark 1:16-20
[2] John 3:16
[3] Philippians 2:5-8

WHAT JESUS SAID ABOUT ...

HIMSELF 'God did not send his Son into the world to condemn the world, but to save the world through him' – John 3:17

HIS MISSION 'I have come that (you) may have life, and have it to the full' – John 10:10

ATTITUDE 'I am among you as one who serves' – Luke 22:27

LOVE 'As I have loved you, so you must love one another' – John 13:34

ACTIONS 'In everything, do to others what you would have them do to you' – Matthew 7:12

CHOICE 'You cannot serve both God and Money' – Matthew 6:24

CONSEQUENCES 'Whatever you did not do for one of the least of these, you did not do for me' – Matthew 25:45

HUMILITY 'Anyone who will not receive the kingdom of God like a little child will never enter it' – Luke 18:17

RECOGNISING GOD 'Blessed are the pure in heart, for they will see God' – Matthew 5:8

TRUTH 'Let your "Yes" be "Yes", and your "No", "No"' – Matthew 5:37 (*NIV 1984*)

FORGIVENESS 'If you forgive other people when they sin against you, your heavenly Father will also forgive you' – Matthew 6:14

JUDGEMENT 'In the same way as you judge others, you will be judged' – Matthew 7:2

HIS LIFE 'No one takes it from me, but I lay it down of my own accord' – John 10:18

HIS DEATH 'God so loved the world that he gave his one and only Son, that whoever believes in him shall not perish but have eternal life' – John 3:16

HIS RESURRECTION 'Because I live, you also will live' – John 14:19

HIS PRESENCE 'I am with you always, to the very end of the age' – Matthew 28:20

About the Author

ROBERT STREET was commissioned a Salvation Army officer with his wife, Janet, in 1969 and, in addition to corps leadership, served as Editor of *The War Cry* for 10 years and also as Editor-in-Chief, United Kingdom Territory. He was Principal, Booth College, London, UK, from 1997-2002 and served on the Army's International Doctrine Council from 2007, retiring as its chairman in 2014. Always keen to work alongside Christians from other denominations, he was chairman of both Norfolk and Suffolk Churches Together during the 1990s, when Divisional Commander, Anglia.

International experience came through service in Australia and appointments that involved oversight of work in the South Pacific and East Asia, as well as Europe, resulting in his seeing Salvation Army ministry in 50 countries. His chairmanship of the International Spiritual Life Commission prompted his writing a number of related books, including *Called to be God's People*, *Servant Leadership* and *Holiness Unwrapped*. More recently he has devised, written and produced the international teaching resource *One Army* of which *Who is this Jesus anyway?* is a part.